HEAVEN AND HELL

HEAVEN AND HELL

VICTOR BOOKS®

A DIVISION OF SCRIPTURE PRESS PUBLICATIONS INC.
USA CANADA ENGLAND

Most Scripture quotations are taken from the *Holy Bible, New International Version*, © 1973, 1978, 1984, International Bible Society. Used by permission of Zondervan Bible Publishers. Other quotations are from *New American Standard Bible* (NASB), © the Lockman Foundation 1960, 1962, 1963, 1968, 1971, 1972, 1973, 1975, 1977.

Recommended Dewey Decimal Classification: 236
Suggested Subject Heading: ESCHATOLOGY

Library of Congress Catalog Card Number: 90-60254
ISBN: 0-89693-768-2

1 2 3 4 5 6 7 8 9 10 Printing/Year 94 93 92 91 90

VICTOR BOOKS
A division of SP Publications, Inc.
Wheaton, Illinois 60187

•CONTENTS•

Recognition to Beth Donigan Seversen
for assistance
in researching and formulating
parts of this book.

• INTRODUCTION •

Is there a heaven—and is there a hell? The answer is—according to Jesus, there is both, and we can understand enough to affect our eternal destiny.

The Bible tells us all we need to know about such things. After all, it is inspired by the One who came back from the dead to inform us about these incredibly important matters. There is a natural curiosity about the afterlife that raises questions this book can help to meet.

• BEFORE YOU BEGIN •

People who gather together for Bible study are likely to be at different places in their spiritual lives, and their study materials should be flexible enough to meet their different needs. This book is designed to be used as a Bible study guide for such groups in homes or churches. It can also be used by individuals who are studying on their own. The lessons are written in five distinct sections, so that they can be used in a variety of situations. Groups and individuals alike can choose to use the elements they find most useful in the order they find most beneficial.

These studies will help you learn some new truths from the Bible as well as how to dig out those truths. You will learn not only *what* the Bible says, but how to use Scripture to deepen your relationship with Jesus Christ by obeying it and applying it in daily living. These studies will also provide an opportunity for potential leaders to learn how to lead a discussion in a nonthreatening setting.

What You'll Need

For each study you will need a Bible and this Bible study guide. You might also want to have a notebook in which to record your thoughts and discoveries from your personal study and group meetings. A notebook could also be used to record prayer requests from the group.

The Sections

Food for Thought. This is a devotional narrative that introduces the topic, person, or passage featured in the lesson. There are several ways it can be used. Each person could read it before coming to the group meeting, and someone could briefly summarize it at the beginning. It could be read silently by each person at the beginning of the session, or it could be read aloud, by one or several group members. (Suggested time: 10 minutes)

Talking It Over. This section contains discussion questions to help you review what you learned in Food for Thought. There are also questions to help you apply the narrative's truths to daily life. The person who leads the discussion of these questions need not be a trained or experienced teacher. All that is needed is someone to keep things moving and facilitate group interaction. (Suggested time: 30 minutes)

Praying It Through. This is a list of suggestions for prayer based on the lesson. You may want to use all the suggestions or eliminate some in order to leave more time for personal sharing and prayer requests. (Suggested time: 20 minutes)

Digging Deeper. The questions in this section are also related to the passage, topic, or character from the lesson. But they will not always be limited to the exact passage or character from Food for Thought. Passages and characters from both the Old and New Testaments will appear in this section, in order to show how God has worked through *all* of history in people's lives. These questions will require a little more thinking and some digging into Scripture, as well as some use of Bible study tools. Participants will be stretched as they become experienced in the "how-tos" of Bible study. (Suggested time: 45 minutes)

Tool Chest. The Tool Chest contains a description of a specific type of Bible study help and includes an explanation of how it is used. An example of the tool is given, and an example of it or excerpt from it is usually included in the Digging Deeper study.

The Bible study helps in the Tool Chest can be purchased by anyone who desires to build a basic library of Bible study reference books and other tools. They would also be good additions to a church library. Some are reasonably inexpensive, but others are quite expensive. A few may be available in your local library or in a seminary or college library. A group might decide to purchase one tool during each series and build a corporate tool chest for all the members of the group to use. You can never be too young a Christian to begin to master Bible study helps, nor can you be too old to learn new methods of rightly dividing the Word of truth.

Options for Group Use

Different groups, made up of people at diverse stages of spiritual growth, will want to use the elements in this book in different ways. Here are a few suggestions to get you started, but be creative and sensitive to your group's needs.

☐ Spend 5–15 minutes at the beginning of the group time introducing yourselves and having group members answer an icebreaker question. (Sample icebreaker questions are included under Tips for Leaders.)

☐ Extend the prayer time to include sharing of prayer requests, praise items, or things group members have learned recently in their times of personal Bible study.

☐ The leader could choose questions for discussion from the Digging Deeper section based on whether participants have prepared ahead of time or not.

☐ The entire group could break into smaller groups to allow different groups to use different sections. (The smaller groups could move to other rooms in the home or church where you are meeting.)

Tips for Leaders

Preparation

1. Pray for the Holy Spirit's guidance as you study, that you will be equipped to teach the lesson and make it appealing and applicable.

2. Read through the entire lesson and any Bible passages or verses that are mentioned. Answer all the questions.

3. Become familiar enough with the lesson that, if time in the group is running out, you know which questions could most easily be left out.

4. Gather all the items you will need for the study: name tags, extra pens, extra Bibles.

The Meeting

1. Start and end on time.

2. Have everyone wear a name tag until group members know one another's names.

3. Have each person introduce himself or herself, or ask regular attenders to introduce guests.

4. For each meeting, pick an icebreaker question or another activity to help group members get to know one another better.

5. Use any good ideas to make everyone feel comfortable.

The Discussion

1. Ask the questions, but try to let the group answer. Don't be afraid of silence. Reword the question if it is unclear to the group or answer it yourself to clarify.

2. Encourage everyone to participate. If someone is shy, ask that person to answer an opinion question or another nonthreatening question. If someone tends to monopolize the discussion, thank that person for his or her contribution and ask if someone else has anything he or she would like to add. (Or ask that person to make the coffee!)

3. If someone gives an incorrect answer, don't bluntly or tactlessly tell him or her so. If it is partly right, reinforce that. Ask if anyone else has any thoughts on the subject. (Disagree agreeably!)

4. Avoid tangents. If someone is getting off the subject, ask that person how his or her point relates to the lesson.

5. Don't feel threatened if someone asks a question you can't answer. Tell the person you don't know but will find out before the next meeting—then be sure to find out! Or ask if someone would like to research and present the answer at the group's next meeting.

Icebreaker Questions

The purpose of these icebreaker questions is to help the people in your group get to know one another over the course of the study. The questions you use when your group members don't know one another very well should be very general and nonthreatening. As time goes on, your questions can become more focused and specific. Always give group members the option of passing if they think a question is too personal.

What do you like to do for fun?
What is your favorite season? dessert? book?
What would be your ideal vacation?
What exciting thing happened to you this week?
What was the most memorable thing you did with your family when you were a child?
What one word best describes the way you feel today?
Tell three things you are thankful for.
Imagine that your house is on fire. What three things would you try to take with you on your way out?
If you were granted one wish, what would it be?
What experience of your past would you most enjoy reliving?

What quality do you most appreciate in a friend?

What is your pet peeve?

What is something you are learning to do or trying to get better at?

What is your greatest hope?

What is your greatest fear?

What one thing would you like to change about yourself?

What has been the greatest accomplishment of your life?

What has been the greatest disappointment of your life?

Need More Help?

Here is a list of books that contain helpful information on leading discussions and working in groups:

> *How to Lead Small Group Bible Studies* (NavPress, 1982).
> *Creative Bible Learning for Adults*, Monroe Marlowe and Bobbie Reed (Regal, 1977).
> *Getting Together*, Em Griffin (InterVarsity Press, 1982).
> *Good Things Come in Small Groups* (InterVarsity Press, 1985).

One Last Thought

This book is a tool you can use whether you have one or one hundred people who want to study the Bible and whether you have one or no teachers. Don't wait for a brilliant Bible study leader to appear—most such teachers acquired their skills by starting with a book like this and learning as they went along. Torrey said, "The best way to begin, is to begin." Happy beginnings!

1
How Do We Get to Heaven?

•FOOD FOR THOUGHT•

Have you ever had to answer a child's questions concerning heaven? Perhaps you have had your own anxious inquiries about a loved one who has died. Have you ever wondered if heaven is really all it is cracked up to be? Maybe you ask yourself if you will like it there, especially if it will just be like an endless Sunday. Most people wonder a little about these things once in a while.

A few years ago, a local newspaper in our city took a telephone poll of people's beliefs. They asked how many believed in God. Ninety-six percent answered in the affirmative. They asked how many believed in heaven and hell. Ninety percent replied that they did. Now ours is known to be a city of churches and churchgoers, but that is a pretty high percentage. If, however, the pollster had continued to ask his questions and inquired *what* these people believed about heaven and hell, he would in all probability have received a huge variety of answers.

All religions have a path that leads to "somewhere," usually to their concept of heaven. All religions purport to provide release. But there is no agreement about what it is a man must be released from. The major religions have their own ideas, of course. Islam believes in a place called heaven where "rivers of milk unchanging in flavor and rivers of wine delight the drinkers" (*Koran*, SURA 47, lines 15-20).

Buddhism's big hope is to "cross over" with others, rather than "crossing over" alone, but they believe that the ultimate bliss is that of "nothingness"; while Hinduism has been described as a big storehouse where all religions and religious experiments can live together. Hindus have a kind of infinite tolerance about any belief about anything; so as far as they are concerned, who knows what heaven is, or who goes there!

Some African religions believe the grave is the seal of everything. That humans become spirits when they die, and that the best that can happen to them then is to become intermediators between God and man. There is no concept of "rest," or being with God forever for these folks.

Judaism believes one's eternal existence in the hereafter is determined by moral behavior and attitudes now. The notion of an afterlife is not very well developed in the Old Testament. In fact, many modern Jews criticize Christians for being selfish, and too concerned with personal eternal rewards.

"Isms" abound. Humanism and existentialism state that heaven is here and now, and we must strive for utopia on earth. Marxism and Atheism believe the Christian concept of heaven is "pie in the sky," choosing rather to reverence the "state" as the object of their hopes and dreams. Cultism, in the form of Jehovah's Witnesses, believes only 144,000 will make it to heaven's glory, while Mormons hold that "every man who reigns in celestial glory is a god to his dominions" (McConkie MD, p. 322). Spiritualism believes life evolves past death toward perfection as man becomes spirit after death, and the New Age thinkers lean toward reincarnation and seem to have as many varied opinions as the Hindus.

But what do Christians believe? Surely we have something specific to say about heaven. The Christian doesn't use his own ingenuity or mere "speculation" to formulate his belief about God, rather he relies on revelation. This is the firm belief that God has revealed Himself to man and that He has spoken in His Word through His prophets in the past, and in these "last days," in His Son Jesus Christ (Hebrews 1:10). In John 14:1-6, Jesus, speaking about heaven, assures His disciples that He is telling them the truth about heaven, and if it were not so, He would have told them! (John 14:2)

The word "heaven" itself implies incomprehensibility because it carries the idea of "concealment." Only He who conceals is able to reveal. " 'No eye has seen, no ear has heard, no mind has conceived what God has prepared for those who love Him,' but God has revealed it to us by His Spirit" (1 Corinthians 2:10). The Christian possesses the Holy Spirit whose work it is to interpret these revelations to us earthlings and help us comprehend what little we are able to comprehend on our own. The Spirit, moreover, works to reveal these things by illuminating the Scriptures for us. So where do we begin to find our answers? Fittingly, in the book of the beginnings—Genesis.

The Egyptians believed that heaven was only for the Pharaohs and their families (those made in their image). They believed Pharaoh was divine. Moses, brought up in Pharaoh's house and taught Pharaoh's religion, destined perhaps for Pharaoh's throne, did not believe the Pharaoh's theology. "Only God is divine, and men and women are made in His image," he said. Even though sin had spoiled the divine likeness, God had made a way to be forgiven through a blood sacrifice so that men and women can go to be with God after death. Moses wrote all this down in his writings and heaven became a thoroughly biblical concept.

But the Bible speaks of heaven in different senses, using the same word, and so we must define the word by its context. It speaks of heaven as the clouds about our heads (Genesis 1:6-8); God is active there. The word is also used for the firmament above the clouds, where the lights of sun, moon, and stars move (Genesis 1:14, 17; 2:1). God is also active there. Then the Bible uses the word heaven to describe a "heavenly experience" of life with Christ now. A sphere of spiritual living that Christ died to make possible and lives to make real (Ephesians 2:6). The "kingdom of heaven" is another expression used in the New Testament to define any sphere where God is King. But then the word is also used to describe the abode of God, or God's home in a particular sense. It is this aspect of the word "heaven" we will be looking into.

So where is this heaven? Some think it is "up." The Hebrew word *shamayim* means "the heights," and in ancient Jewish thought and primitive Christianity, the thought was that heaven indeed was "up there" somewhere. Verses like Isaiah 66:1: "This is what the Lord says: 'Heaven is My throne, and the earth is My footstool,' " lent credence to that thought. God was conceived of as above and coming down. Jesus ascended "up," while Stephen being martyred for his faith, looked "up." Heaven is obviously beyond "up." It's more a state—another dimension. Kittle says you can't ask "where" heaven is, as that opposes the whole concept which is "concealment." We should rather ask, "if" heaven "is." The answer to that is most definitely "yes." Heaven *is*, and heaven, Jesus told us, is where God is! And so, we should strive to understand the concept rather than debate the location of God's abode.

Jesus, well aware of our earthly minds struggling to understand heavenly things, gave an illustration that we can all relate to. The Lord had just told His grieving disciples He was leaving them to return to His Heavenly Father. He comforted them by telling them He was going "home." Now all of them could relate to that! They had left homes and loved ones to follow Him. How they must have longed to go "home" themselves. They knew they could all find their way back to their homes, but when Jesus said they should also know the way to His home, they were puzzled. Jesus had said He was going home to "heaven," not home to Nazareth, so as Thomas put it—"we don't know where you are going, so how can we know the way?"

Jesus, in essence, explained that He was the only way to the heavenly home. They needed to follow Him closely as His disciples to get there. He had told them the truth about heaven and He assured them He would give them eternal life so that they too could look forward to living in such a heavenly environment (John 14:6). For those of us living today, knowing Christ is the key. Receiving His risen life "now" means living with Him "then." As John puts it, "And this is the testimony: God has given us eternal life, and this life is in His Son. He who has the Son has life; he who does not have the Son of God does not have life" (1 John 5:11-12).

Now this information about heaven was meant to comfort the disciples' hearts. They were afraid. They were about to lose someone they loved, and yet here was that same beloved one telling them He was going to go ahead of them to His Father's house in order to prepare rooms in that heavenly home for them as well—and not only for them, but for all who would believe in Him through their testimony (John 17:20).

The picture Jesus used was that of an inn. A lodging place of safety, rest, and refreshment. God was like the innkeeper and Jesus Himself would live permanently there. After explaining this, Jesus promised He would come again and receive them to Himself so that they could all be together forever. Jesus comes for us at death, and for some He will come at His second coming. Whenever He comes, the idea is to be ready.

When my husband and I moved into a condominium two years ago, the carpet salesman came to show me his samples. "This one will last you fifty years," he said proudly. "We haven't got 50 years," I answered. "Sell us the one that will last 25 years—then we are probably moving!" He was somewhat taken aback! I thought about my words too. It was quite a thought that our present home will in all likelihood be the last house we will live in here on earth. Where we are going we won't need carpet—the rooms are paved with gold!!

Another thought that is a comfort is that Jesus said the disciples will be there too! He said, "That there 'you' may be also." Will we know each other when we all get to our heavenly home? Oh, yes!

"You" is plural, and so we shall surely know those we know here. What joy!

First Thessalonians 4 tells of Jesus coming to earth at the Second Coming. Paul says He will bring those we mourn who have died in the Lord with Him, so that together "with them" we shall be ever with the Lord. This very passage of Scripture was written with "comfort" of heart in view. "Wherefore 'comfort' one another with these words," Paul says in 1 Thessalonians 4:18, KJV. Death is never a final separation for those who know Christ. It is merely a parenthesis, a time lapse. One day we shall all be together again!

•TALKING IT OVER•

Suggested Times

1. REVIEW MAN'S SPECULATION.
   Review what the following believe about heaven:
   ☐ Buddhists
   ☐ Hindus
   ☐ Muslims
   ☐ Humanists
   ☐ Marxists
   ☐ New Age Thinkers

5 minutes

2. EXAMINE GOD'S REVELATION.
   ☐ Write a sentence about the different types of heaven spoken about in the Bible.
   A. Genesis 1:6-8

   B. Genesis 1:14-15

   C. Ephesians 2:6

   ☐ Share something new you learned about heaven today and what difference it will make in your life.

10 minutes

5 minutes

3. DISCUSS CHRIST'S SALVATION.
   ☐ How do we get to heaven? Read John 14:1-6. What do you think is the *most* important thing Jesus said in these verses? How can we be sure? Examine 1 John 5:11-12.

10 minutes

•PRAYING IT THROUGH•

Suggested Times

1. (In twos) Praise God for
   ☐ His goodness.
   ☐ a heaven to go to.
   ☐ a way to get there.

5 minutes

2. (In twos) Fill in the acrostic below with concepts of heaven. Then pray for someone who needs this hope.

   H - Healing
   E
   A
   V
   E
   N

5 minutes

3. (As a group) Pray for:
   ☐ millions who have no hope in heaven.
   ☐ millions who have false hopes of heaven.
   ☐ the church worldwide as it preaches the truth in Jesus.
   ☐ those that mourn "as those who have no hope."
   ☐ those in the family of God recently bereaved.
   ☐ those lacking in the assurance of their salvation.

5 minutes

4. (On your own) Praise God for your own personal salvation.

5 minutes

•DIGGING DEEPER•

John 14:1-7

1. Read John 14:1-7. Jesus, we observe, is consoling the disciples. What is the setting for His words of comfort?

    13:1-5

    13:21

    13:33

    13:36-38

2. How does the setting help us understand Christ's words in 14:1?

3. What twofold remedy is here given for a troubled heart? See also Psalms 4:5; 115:9; Proverbs 3:5; 28:26; Isaiah 26:4.

4. What are the implications behind Jesus suggesting that His disciples trust in Him?

5. Find the key or repeated words and phrases in this passage. Explain why they are emphasized.

6. Jesus is saving a "special place" in His Father's house (heaven, or eternity) for His disciples. If you are one of His disciples, knowing this promise, how do you feel?

7. Let's analyze Jesus' argument, or line of thinking in verses 1-7. What is His premise or thesis statement? How does He support it? Does Jesus use inductive or deductive reasoning here?

8. How would you describe the nature of the place Jesus refers to in this passage?

9. Prompted by Thomas' concern, Jesus made certain the disciples knew how to get there. How can we attain heaven?

10. Reread verses 1-7. What do Jesus' comments reveal about His own relationship with the Father?

11. Are you troubled today? How can Christ's teaching about heaven bring you hope and comfort?

For Further Study
  1. Read the Word Commentary on John 14:1-7. How does it add to your understanding of this passage?
  2. Memorize John 14:1-2. Have a friend quiz you.

•TOOL CHEST•
(A Suggested Optional Resource)

WORD BIBLICAL COMMENTARY, VOLUME 36, John (Word Books)
Commentaries should be consulted only after you have first done your own study of a particular passage. The rule, allow Scripture to interpret Scripture, is an important guideline to enforce in your personal study habits. When you have a question, or come to a difficult word, phrase, or verse to interpret, first examine the surrounding context. Often the answer is just around the next verse. If you still cannot determine the meaning or are unsure of the answer to your question, turn to a good commentary for help. When I think of using a commentary, the checks and balances analogy comes to mind. I pick up a commentary to check out the conclusion I have drawn after my personal study. If my answer appears way off from the scholars then I restudy the passage and/or observe a few other commentators' opinions noting their supporting arguments.

Good commentaries are those which offer sound scriptural support for their conclusions and which you find yourself consulting frequently. If you are uncomfortable with a commentary's theological persuasion, style, or terminology, you will find it sits on your shelf gathering dust.

George R. Beasley-Murray's *The Word Biblical Commentary* on John is worth your perusal. All the volumes are not necessarily of the same caliber, so do borrow a friend's or your church library's before making your purchase.

2
What Is Heaven Like?

•FOOD FOR THOUGHT•

What is heaven like? Is it a place, or a state? If a place, where is it located? If another dimension, what does that mean? We struggle to make sense of things that as yet make no sense to us at all! And yet, if heaven is a concept Christ talked about, then we should talk about it too. If Paul said he had a "desire to depart and be with Christ which is better by far," then we should have a desire to look into those things that come after death (Philippians 1:23).

I remember shortly after my mother died, an Anglican priest who had had a huge part to play in my own life sent me a little poem:

> Better to be a lark on high
> Singing for joy 'gainst a cloudless sky
> Better to know no sorrow or pain
> No darkness or death,
> But to live again.

> Better to breathe in Heaven's pure air
> A lamb that is safe in the Shepherd's care
> Better, far better with Christ to be
> Living and loved through eternity.
>
> R.E. Cleeve

It is very hard to believe it is "better, far better" when your father's body lies laid out, shunned and cold on the bed upstairs! There's dread involved when death comes knocking at the door.

We need to realize first of all that death is a dreadful thing! The act of dying is not pretty. All of us may be forgiven for dreading the process of dying, but we must endure the pain, looking ahead to the release of the spirit from the body.

Some years ago, I was asked to tour a hospital. We began by looking at the gynecological ward. Babies burped, screamed, stretched, and gurgled. It was such a happy place! At the end of the tour, we walked through the hospice. How different the atmosphere!

"I see this is your birthing wing," I observed to my guide.

The hospital official indulgently smiled. "No, no, this is the hospice. We began in the birthing wing!"

"I beg to differ," I replied. "*This* is the birthing wing! Here the spirit struggles to be born into the afterlife as surely as the baby struggles to be born into this life!"

The official gave me a strange look, but I happen to believe that statement is true!

What happens at the moment of death? The spirit wings its way to God! Jesus said He would come again for us. If we die before that particular promise is fulfilled, He will come for us on our death bed.

I derive great peace and comfort from the words of Jesus to the thief from the cross: "Today" [not tomorrow, or as some believe months after our spirit wanders the netherworld aimlessly] you will be with me in paradise" (Luke 23:43). When my mother died and my sister and I buried her, my sister suggested I choose some words for the gravestone. This was the text I chose: "Absent from the body and at home with the Lord" (2 Corinthians 5:8, NASB). If you have ever seen a dead body you will know in truth the first part of that verse is right! The person is gone. He or she is very definitely absent from the body! But it is the second part of that verse we need to know in truth if we are to derive help at these times. Are our loved ones present with the Lord? We prayed. Yes, we told them or tried to tell them they needed to trust God, but did they? We agonize and wonder and weep and wring our hands. We need to know, and yet we cannot know. But there is something we can do. We can trust God that He heard our prayers and answered them!

So often there is an eternal awareness of impending death borne upon a dying soul that alerts them to the coming event. When my father died, the doctors decided it was in his best interest to withhold that information from him. In fact, they believed he would only fight the disease if he were encouraged to believe he would recover. I was instructed not to tell him. And yet, he knew! I suppose when you are dying you are bound to know! A few days before his death, he put his affairs in order and put his business into his son-in-law's hands. Prayers get answered, God whispers into our inner ear, "You're coming home," and we *know*. Never shortchange what the

Holy Spirit does in answer to your prayers for a dying person. Be assured He is busy! And don't be afraid to pray with them and as opportunity comes, share the Christian hope of heaven. And it is a hope! A glorious confidence that it is far better than the best that earth can give. Don't underestimate the concern of Christ and the work of His love through His church for your friends you think don't know the Lord. I was amazed to hear at my friend's funeral the people Christ had sent her way from the little church down the way. His people are everywhere—on TV, radio, sending their messages through books and tracts, and spoken words of kindness and little deeds of love! And when there are no human witnesses, God says His stars tell His glory and His world His story—He has not left Himself speechless!

In the Book of Revelation, the Apostle John had a vision. He says he saw a door standing open in heaven. He saw many things through that door. He tried to describe in symbol and picture with meager human vocabulary what heaven is like. We can look over his shoulder—and we should! A dying man using the picture of the door open in heaven said, "God's finger is on the latch and I am ready for Him to open the door." It is prudent, however, to look through the door of Scripture before God's finger is on the latch!

Heaven is heavily populated, and yet there is room for everyone who lives there. It is certainly a sizable place. It has many rooms. Seeing there will be a great multitude which no man can number living there (Revelation 7:9), it's encouraging to know there will be no problem of overcrowding. When Jesus said, "How dare you turn My Father's house into a market!" (John 2:16) He used the same word as in John 14:2 when He said, "In my Father's house are many rooms." This prepared place that belonged to His Father was not only likened to the family home, but to the temple. The temple was huge. It had many courts, chambers, porches, and walkways. No matter how many thronging worshipers there were in the earthly temple in Jerusalem, it always had more room for the crowds. This represents in some little way the spatial spaciousness of our heavenly home. There will be space to breathe and room to grow!

The house or temple is described in terms we can relate to. The Bible speaks of gates. Gates say, among other things, that the place they guard belongs to someone! And heaven indeed belongs to God. Christ purchased the house behind the gates by giving His life—shedding His blood, on the cross.

There is an old legend of magic gates that refused all who tried to force them open. Yet if one drop of blood touched them, they flew open at once. What a picture of heaven's gates, opened by the Son's death!

There is not only access to our room in the Father's mansion because of Christ's death on our behalf, but we shall receive the most personal of welcomes. "I am going there to prepare a place for you," said Jesus (John 14:3). Even though most believe Jesus is speaking of the Second Coming, none would argue the fact that the disciples to whom He was speaking, and all the rest of us who will die before He comes again, want to know if He will come for us too! I believe the Bible teaches that Jesus will be personally involved, not only in the preparation in heaven for us, but Jesus will personally receive us at death! Christ will not trust our soul to all the angels of heaven. This is not to denigrate the wonderful ministering spirits who will attend Him and us at the point of our departure, but rather to emphasize the personal nature of Christ's care for us in death!

Another picture that helps us to visualize the migration of the soul is Paul's picture of the tent. "We know," says Paul, "that if the earthly tent we live in is destroyed, we have a building from God, an eternal house in heaven, not built by human hands" (2 Corinthians 5:1). For those of us with a few pegs missing, that's a great picture! To dismantle this tent and pitch a new tent in heaven for us is a graphic visual aid—unless you detest camping!

Perhaps the fruit, rivers, and combination of colors promised will intrigue those of an ascetic nature, or the soothing words, "They shall hunger and thirst no more," will beckon the undernourished of our planet, or those who don't know what pure water looks like, but certainly all of us can relate to the fact that there is no first aid station, intensive care unit, or health clinics in heaven! "No more pain," the Bible says. Joni Earickson Tada, a prisoner in her wheelchair will dance then! We are told 90 percent of the people in the world will die without a doctor's help. "No more pain" will sound pretty good to them if we ever get around to telling them the good news of the Gospel!

There will, moreover, be no more sorrow, nor crying, for "God shall wipe away all tears from our eyes." What tears are these and how can they be shed in heaven? That is a mystery.

Perhaps they will be fresh on our cheeks as we arrive crying from the birthing wing—born into the rarefied air of our new environment. Or maybe they will be tears of sorrow that the family circle is broken and loved ones are not there. Whatever these tears represent, God will wipe them away forever, for we shall by some miracle know no sorrow!

But what of the people we will meet again? Will we recognize them? Jesus said, "You shall be with Me" (John 14:3). Paul promised a reunion in the air with those redeemed who have died (1 Thessalonians 4:17). The disciples saw Moses and Elijah talking with Jesus on the Mount of Transfiguration and recognized those who had been long dead instantly.

Yes, it will be a prepared place, a purchased place, a pretty place, a permanent place, but above all it will be a people place. Populated with people who have been forgiven of their sins and live in the power of an endless life. Will you be there? Make sure now by receiving Christ.

You may make this prayer your own if you wish:

> Dear Lord, I believe You died to make it possible for me to go to heaven. It was Your death that opened heaven's gates. Forgive my sins that made Your death necessary, and come into my heart by Your Spirit, that endless life may be mine.
> Amen.

•TALKING IT OVER•

1. READ.   *5 minutes*
   Read Philippians 1:23. Why is it far better to depart and be with Christ? Be specific. Then read Revelation 1:10-17.

2. DISCUSS.   *20 minutes*
   Make a list of the things John saw when he saw the living risen Christ. (For example, He was dressed in a robe going down to his feet.) After making your list, discuss what each symbol means.
   ☐ What was the result of this vision? (v. 17)
   ☐ What were the names Jesus used for Himself and what do you think is the significance? (v. 17)

3. CONSIDER YOUR OWN EXPERIENCE.   *5 minutes*
   Having discussed this risen, glorified Saviour, what does this say about our experience with Him in heaven?

•PRAYING IT THROUGH•

Suggested Times

1. (As a group) Praise God for promising us a body in heaven (2 Corinthians 5:1). Praise Him also for all the other promises He gives us concerning the afterlife.

10 minutes

2. (On your own) Pray for people who do not yet know Christ whom you would like to live in a room of the Father's house in heaven.

5 minutes

3. (In twos) Pray for nominal Christians who would like to go to heaven but don't know for certain they will. Then take a personal moment to praise God for your salvation.

5 minutes

•DIGGING DEEPER•

2 Corinthians 5:1-10

1. Read 2 Corinthians 5:1-10. What is the dominant thought in verses 1-5?

2. Study the preceding context (2 Corinthians 4:7-18). Identify the main point.

3. How does our passage, 2 Corinthians 5:1-10, fit with the preceding context?

4. What encouragement would Paul's readers find from his letter?

5. Describe our heavenly dwelling.

6. Explain verse 5.

7. What is the tone of this passage? Note the repetition in verses 6 and 8.

8. Do you share Paul's confidence and his preference? (cf., v. 8; Philippians 1:23; Luke 23:43; Revelation 7:9; 1 Thessalonians 4:17)

9. What will be judged at the Judgment Seat of Christ?

10. What is your outlook on suffering and death? How can you become more like Paul? (cf., 1 Corinthians 11:1)

11. What do you think Paul's purpose was for including these 10 verses?

12. How do you need to prepare yourself for the Judgment Seat of Christ?

For Further Study
1. Are you afraid of death? If so, in a journal, write yourself a letter of consolation based on this Scripture passage.
2. Memorize 2 Corinthians 5:8-9.

•TOOL CHEST•
(A Suggested Optional Resource)

SEARCH THE SCRIPTURES

Is your daily devotional life suffering the doldrums? Would you like to develop good Bible study methods? *Search the Scriptures* (IVP) can enhance both these areas for you. This devotional is an inductive approach to systematically reading and studying the entire Bible in three years. The daily reading assignment is followed by two or three inductive questions for you to answer. An introduction and an outline are provided for each book of the Bible. Study notes are also included where background information is helpful for interpreting the passage. Feel free to follow the suggested reading plan, or try beginning with a book of the Bible with which you feel least comfortable. *Search the Scriptures* can satisfy that yearning you have had for a fresh approach to daily devotions.

3

The Resurrection of the Body

•FOOD FOR THOUGHT•

John Richard Moreland caught the joy of resurrection morning when he wrote:

Resurrection

Since One, for love, died on a tree
And in the stony
Tomb has lain,
Behold I show a mystery:
All sepulchres
Are sealed in vain!

From *A Blue Wave Breaking*

We can know all sepulchres are indeed sealed in vain. We who trust, "he that believeth in Him shall never die," can have confidence that we ourselves shall be with the Lord and our bodies will be raised at the last day. John Richard Moreland died in 1947. He found his sepulchre sealed in vain—and so shall we!

There is a finality to death that crushes the spirit and leaves one breathless with sorrows unless you are a Christian.

Jesus promised we would be with Him in His Father's house (John 14:1-2). The moment a believer's soul leaves his body he enters into the good of that promise. "Absent from the body, he is *present* with the Lord" (2 Corinthians 5:8). This belief should comfort the grieving family and friends that are left behind. If we thought those we loved were in *soul sleep* or suspended in some sort of unconscious state somewhere, we would experience sorrow upon sorrow. Some of the most helpful things I have been able to say to people who have been bereaved have been to assure them that at that very moment of intense grief, their loved one is more alive than they have ever been, healthier than they could ever experience on earth, and happier than they have ever dreamed possible.

Not only does this comfort a grieving relative, but helps to alleviate guilt. Sometimes when death occurs suddenly without the parties being able to prepare for it—there can be a lot of unfinished business to feel guilty about. Perhaps there were harsh words that should never have been spoken, or actions that needed to be forgiven. Maybe responsibilities were neglected. Cicely Saunders says, "We must not lose the chance of making good on a great deal of untidiness in our lives, or of making time to pack our bags and say, 'Sorry, goodbye and thank you' " (*Time*, September 5, 1988, p. 58). But how many of us follow her advice? What joy to know our loved one has forgiven us because they are made perfect! When my mother died, I struggled with a lot of guilt because I hadn't shared more of my Christian faith with her. I played the "if only" game over and over again. The pastor who officiated at her funeral helped me to realize my guilt was somewhat self-centered and I should be rejoicing in the fact that even if I wasn't happy—she was! She was being comforted by the Lord in the conscious presence of the Father and His angels, not to mention her beloved husband and parents. I was greatly challenged that day to read Philippians 4:4, "Rejoice in the Lord *always* and again I say rejoice," and wrote the following in my prayer diary:

> "Always" Lord—"always"—even now? That's hard!
> I had the chance, and I didn't take it;
> I had the prayers, and I didn't pray them;
> I had the love, and I didn't give it.
> I had the words, and I didn't say them!
>
> But!—God had the chance, and He was taking it;
> He had the prayers, and He was praying them;
> He had the love, and He was giving it;
> He had the words, and He was saying them!

Sometimes I'm overwhelmed with a great hunger for a sight of her, a touch of her. Then I remember where she is and I seem to imagine her saying, "You shouldn't feel my loss so much. You know where I am and who I'm with. Sooner than you know, you will be here too!" I know one thing. She doesn't want me to carry the guilt of "all I didn't do," so I leave it at the empty tomb and rejoice! Thank You, Lord—I can and will rejoice in that!

I know I would have experienced a lot of problems if I had believed my mother's soul was merely "sleeping."

Someone has said that when the spirit leaves our body at the time of death, our body awaits the resurrection while our souls are "at this moment in a chamber of the Father's house." That is a most comforting thought.

But what will our resurrection body be like? Will it resemble a reanimated corpse? In a paper on the subject of immortality, Murray Harris says that the resurrection will be more than reanimation. It will not be decomposed corpses reassembled with the same atomic structure as our present bodies. In other words, Harris argues for the "receipt of a new body" as a permanent home of the soul and not "a standing up of corpses."

Christ's resurrection body is the prototype for our own. When Jesus was raised from the dead His body had powers that ours have not. He could walk through locked doors and vanish, and then reappear at will. Yet Thomas was invited to thrust his fingers into hands that had holes in them to convince him this was indeed "the same Jesus" he had accompanied for three years! He was the same, yet different. Recognizable—if He wished, for example when He appeared in the Upper Room. Yet if He wanted—"hidden"; for example—His appearance to the two disciples on the road to Emmaus. Clearly Jesus' resurrection body was beyond the limits that His earthly body had been subject to. Our bodies like His will not be bound by time or space. Philippians 3:21 says, "[Jesus] will transform our lowly bodies so that they will be like His glorious body."

The body of the resurrection is described as "a spiritual body" by Paul (1 Corinthians 15:44b). It is also called an incorruptible, beautiful, powerful, celestial body.

But, you say, what will it really be like? Somehow I was hoping for a change of body rather than "the same old one but different." Some of us that have struggled with accepting the bodies we have been given for earth may not be terribly enthralled with the idea of another one quite like it for eternity! First Corinthians 15 tells us that even as our finite minds cannot grasp our infinite destiny, so those same finite minds cannot anticipate that infinite gift of a spiritual resurrection body! Paul uses the realm of nature to help us to grasp an infinitesimal part of the truth of it. He says our heavenly body will be as superior as the flower to the bulb! That's a good picture. Think of a daffodil bulb. Then think of the flower. Could there be any comparison between them? Yet both are unmistakably daffodil in nature. One belongs to the earth and is totally suitable for its environment. But the flower of the bulb dances in the fresh air and sunlight above the ground, totally suited to its environment.

Paul, a tent maker, uses another pertinent illustration. In 2 Corinthians 5:1-11 he talks about his earthly tent (that is his body) being destroyed. This doesn't phase him at all as he anticipates his spirit pitching camp and moving into a heavenly tent "not made with hands." During his lifetime Paul's strong hands must have made many a tent, but his heavenly tent had been prepared in an altogether superior way and would be sheer joy to occupy! As our earthly tents begin to lose their tent pegs, the guy ropes slacken and rents appear in their structure. As my body grows older, I am inclined to take great comfort in the Apostle Paul's words!

•TALKING IT OVER•

1. READ.   *10 minutes*
   Read 1 Corinthians 15:36-49. Make a list of all the things this passage teaches us about our:

Earthly Bodies	Spiritual Bodies

2. DISCUSS.   *10 minutes*
   Discuss a new thought arising from your study.

3. STUDY IN TWOS.   *8 minutes*
   Read 2 Corinthians 5:1-11. Which verses comfort you? Which verses challenge you? Which verses chill you? Share your findings with the group.

4. PRAY.   *2 minutes*
   Pray about the things that worry you.

• PRAYING IT THROUGH •

Suggested Times

1. (As a group) Praise God for Christ's resurrection and its implications.

   4 minutes

2. (In twos) Pray for people who have been bereaved. Pray a verse for them from one of the passages in Talking It Through.

   4 minutes

3. (In twos) Pray for people who are dying that some of these facts may comfort them. Ask God if you are the one to speak a word to them.

   4 minutes

4. (On your own) Meditate on the resurrection body God promises you. Thank Him for these promises.

   4 minutes

5. (As a group) Pray for people who are not afraid of dying—but should be! Pray they find Christ.

   4 minutes

•DIGGING DEEPER•

John 14:1-7

1. Study 1 Corinthians 15:35-49. What questions does Paul answer? What does he consider foolish?

Acts 17:32

2. What principle is Paul illustrating in verses 37-41?

Analogy One:

Analogy Two:

Analogy Three:

Principle:

3. Describe the dissimilarities between our earthly and resurrection bodies (vv. 42-44).

Earthly Body	Resurrection Body

4. Read 1 Corinthians 15:45-58. Identify the argument Paul is making in verse 44b. In the following verses, what proofs does he use to support his argument?

5. What assurance does Paul give for the certainty of our receiving a resurrection body?

6. Verse 58 is the punch line of the passage, the so what, or more accurately the *now what*. In knowledge of the fact that we shall receive this marvelous immortal body and victory over death and sin (v. 57), what is to be our response?

7. What situations might you face in the future where recalling these truths could be an encouragement to you?

For Further Study
1. Select a verse from 1 Corinthians 15:35-58 that is meaningful to you and commit it to memory.
2. Write a summary description of the resurrection body in your journal after reviewing the Digging Deeper sections of chapters 2–3.

•TOOL CHEST•
(A Suggested Optional Resource)

THE CROSS OF CHRIST
John Stott's masterpiece, *The Cross of Christ* (IVP), is his most arresting work to date. After reading *The Cross of Christ*, you will never think theology boring again. The section subtitled "The Victory of Christ" is an exciting treatment of our subject of Christ's victory over death and sin. Stott also adequately explains what it means poetically to enter into Christ's victory and to share in His resurrection. This superb work is worthy of your personal or small group study and an exceptional gift for your pastor or elder.

4

The Great Divorce

•FOOD FOR THOUGHT•

James Burtchaell of the University of Notre Dame said, "Heaven and hell are no longer thought of as different locations with separate zip codes, but radically opposed states of intimacy with, and alienation from God" (*Newsweek*, March 27, 1989, p. 52). Alienation is a terrible thing. Nations are alienated from nations, wives from husbands, children from parents, neighbors from neighbors, friends from friends. Alienation brings suffering and often the death of a relationship.

Divorced people know what alienation is all about. But the gravest alienation that there is, is the divorce between God and man because of sin. If we are not reconciled to God in this life, we will certainly not have a chance of reconciliation in the next (Hebrews 9:27). Christ came to give us eternal life and reconciliation is possible because of the Cross.

Jesus taught us the necessity of preparing for the prepared place He has prepared for us! This preparation can begin today. The writer of the Book of Hebrews said, *"Today* is the day of salvation" (Hebrews 3:7). Jesus also talked in parables and directly about hell. A parable is a heavenly story with an earthly meaning. One of the parables concerns a rich man who kept heaping up riches for himself. He thought he had all the time in the world to enjoy them. God calls such a temporal philosophy of living "foolish." "People are fools," says God, "who think they have accumulated great wealth by their own ability and that that is all there is to life." Such people are most unwise, because God summons our souls whenever He wishes! When the night comes that God requires our soul, who is going to argue? In the words of Emily Dickinson:

> Because I could not stop for death
> He kindly stopped for me.

> The carriage held but just ourselves
> And immortality!

One day death will "kindly stop for me" and thee! Whether we take kindly to the truth of that or not is somewhat irrelevant.

So we speculate! Some of us decide to take our chances. We have our doubts about heaven but we have many more doubts about the existence of hell and somehow believe it will all come out right in the end! After all, the argument goes, a good God would surely not send a "nice" person [like me] to a horrid eternal doom. Even if there is such a place, God is all-powerful and therefore can save from punishment those people who have sincerely done the best they can with their lives.

In the film *Coming to America*, Eddie Murphy's character, a rich prince, desires to choose his own wife. Instead of bowing to his country's tradition and allowing his father to choose his bride, the prince travels to America, falls in love with the lowly daughter of the manager of a hamburger joint, and faces his father's wrath. The king is all-powerful. It is now up to him to keep his word and guard tradition. The queen, seeing the young couple really love each other, suggests that, seeing the king *is* all-powerful, he has the power to change his mind or his own decrees, and so he does and the story ends happily ever after.

But we must be careful to realize that this is fantasy from Hollywood and Eddie Murphy's film father is *not* God Almighty—a holy, righteous, heavenly Being. Hell is not a tradition, it is a fact, and God will not change His mind about it. He has told us it will not disappear with a wave of our wish wand.

Martin Marty, a church historian said, "Hell disappeared and no one noticed" (*Newsweek*, March 27, 1989, p. 52). He was referring to the modern liberal ideas that abound in the church. According to the same Newsweek article, "Today hell is theology's 'H' word—a subject too trite for serious scholarship." I'm sure the devil bought up the overrun of *that* magazine for the occupants of hell!

The major religions still purport to believe in hell. The Hindus have a variety of spectacular hells, each with its own exquisite torture. "As a punishment for adultery," says the author of *Other Peoples' Myths*, "a sinner may be forced to embrace a beautiful woman whose temperature is white hot"! "Some Jews," says Rabbi Daniel Landes, "have been through the Holocaust! There's just no need to talk about hell." On the other hand, Islam is much nearer the Christian's belief. After death each person must walk the path, the bridge that stretches over hell. The damned will fall off into the fiery pits of hell! (*Newsweek*, March 27, 1989, p. 52)

Perhaps our modern minds revolt at such medieval mind photos. But a bigger problem for the thinking person is the whole concept of a good God allowing such a place or state of eternal torment to exist at all.

How could a just God justify it? Even if we can accept that some rapists, child abusers, Nazis, and torturers deserve such an end, what about good people? Really good people—like Ghandi for instance? The thing we need to do is first of all realize that hell was not prepared by God for man. It was prepared for the devil and his angels (Matthew 25:41).

But think of the character of Christ another may expostulate. "Didn't Christ tell us to love our enemies? If He loves His enemies, how could He send them to hell?" Christ talked more about hell than most! He definitely believed in its existence. He said we should take the subject seriously and fear being dismissed from God's presence and cast into outer darkness where there will be weeping and gnashing of teeth (Matthew 8:12; 10:28). These are very strong figures of speech that we ignore at our peril! We were told by our Saviour not to fear man or devils, but rather to fear the God who *will* dismiss the unsaved to such a place. In fact, nowhere in the Bible are we told to fear the devil, but rather we are exhorted to fear God!

Having said this, we must still realize that Satan is a formidable foe. Even though he does not reign in hell as literature has led us to believe, and he will be tormented there forever and ever (Revelation 14:4; 20:10) this satanic being has no intention of being lonely! He is, according to Jesus, a liar, deceiver, and a murderer. Paul uses graphic language to describe him, calling him a roaring lion prowling around looking for victims. The devil blinds people's eyes to spiritual realities, but Christ can open those same blind eyes in order to save us. In fact, we must never lose sight of the fact that Jesus overcame the devil and will one day cast him into the "lake of fire" where the "smoke of his torment will rise up forever" (Revelation 14:11).

In short, hell is where Satan and his angels reside, while heaven is God's abode. Hell was prepared for the devil and his followers, while heaven was prepared for "whosoever will come" and drink the water of salvation.

Jesus told us He had come to save lost souls so that they would not keep the devil company for all eternity! Now I wish hell did not exist, that it wasn't true, but I believe with all my heart it is! In fact, if wishing would do anything on my part alone, hell would certainly disappear! Thinking on the subject I tried to imagine myself after death having neglected to accept God's only way of salvation. What would I do if I ended up at the pearly gates with nothing but a wish wand? And I wrote . . . .

The Wish Wand

I had a little wish wand and waved it to and fro
Whenever thoughts turned heavenward
or the other place you go.
I thought it safe to trust it
with my whole eternal soul
so I wished the life I'd lived on earth
would get me to my goal.

I wished that all would get to heaven
whatever they believed
that Buddha sat at God's right hand
that New Age be received.
I wished that Paul would change his mind
that Jesus wasn't right
because He spoke of lostness and a
dark eternal night;
about the way to heaven
one truth, one narrow gate, and
I was so broadminded that I wished away my fate!

So I waved my little wish wand
in the radiant face of Him
who met me at the gate of heaven and wouldn't let me in.
I wrote to heaven's congressman,
but he courteously replied that I should have
left my wish wand at the feet of Him who died!
For wishes could not wish away a lifetime of
rejection,
and wishes could not dress my soul
in heaven's own perfection.
And wishes could not save me now
for hell was so obscene,
that wishes there die ghastly deaths,
strangled with a scream.

So I took my little wish wand
into hell the day I died,
and I waved it at the serpent as he
slithered to my slide.
It was dark but I could see him
and all I knew was fear,
and no matter how I waved my wand
he wouldn't disappear!
Oh I wish that I had wished aright
I wished I lived again
I wished I had a body that
was whole, not racked with pain.
I wished I could remember
something other than the dirt.
I wished I could forget my sin.
so every memory hurt
Oh, I wished and wished and wished
that I could have another chance
to cast upon the Crucified
a trusting, saving glance.

But the devil took my wish wand
and he laughed right in my face
and I went to live eternally in
darkness and disgrace,
I never wished a wish again
I had no heart to try
for hell is where hope ended,
and where all my wishes died!

Wishing will not wish away eternal truths. But remember: "God so loved the world that He gave His one and only Son, that whoever believes in Him shall not perish but have eternal life" (John 3:16). Therefore—choose life! Thank Christ for dying for you and invite Him to forgive your sins and rule your life.

•TALKING IT OVER•

Suggested
Times

1. IDENTIFY.   *5 minutes*
   Circle the objection that is closest to your own
   concerning the existence of hell:
   ☐ the character of God
   ☐ the statements of Scripture
   ☐ the lurid symbolism of the Bible that appears
      outmoded
   ☐ the loving nature of Christ
   ☐ other

2. DISCUSS.   *5 minutes*
   Read Luke 12:16ff. What does this teach you
   about:
   ☐ God?
   ☐ The Rich Man?
   ☐ Yourself?

3. READ.   *10 minutes*
   Read these two passages of Scripture (Ezekiel
   28:11-17, Isaiah 14:12-15). Many theologians believe that Satan can be discerned as the motivat-
   ing force behind these two kings and that the
   passages tell us things about him. Make a list of
   those things from these Scriptures.

4. Read John 3:16 and thank God for the Good   *10 minutes*
   News!

•PRAYING IT THROUGH•

Suggested Times

1. (On your own) Praise God for His □ majesty □ power □ holiness □ victory over Satan	*3 minutes*
2. (As a group) Praise God for Christ's cross where He bruised the serpent's head (Genesis 3:15).	*2 minutes*
3. (As a group) Pray for people you know who seem blind to these spiritual realities and do not believe: □ in hell □ in Satan □ that they are lost	*3 minutes*
4. (In twos) Pray for: □ areas of the world still in the grip of Satan □ the indigenous church in those lands □ missions and missionaries	*2 minutes*
5. (As a group) Pray that God's Spirit will influence our young people on the college campuses, and that Satan-worship may be shown up for what it is.	*5 minutes*
6. (On your own) Make sure *you* know Christ has saved you from hell and will take you to heaven. Ask Him in prayer to forgive your sins and give you assurance of your salvation.	*5 minutes*

•DIGGING DEEPER•

1. What are some pictures the Bible uses to describe hell?

   Matthew 18:9; Mark 9:43-48

   Matthew 8:12; 2 Peter 2:17

   Matthew 25:46

   Matthew 7:21-23; 2 Thessalonians 1:9

   Revelation 2:11

   Revelation 9:1

2. What do the above passages suggest about hell?

3. Who currently inhabits hell?

   2 Peter 2:4

   Jude 6

   Jude 7

   Jude 10–13

   Revelation 9:1-6

   Revelation 11:7

4. In the future, who will inhabit hell and for how long?

   Matthew 25:41

   Revelation 20:7-10, 13-15

5. Why did hell originate and whose idea was it? (Matthew 25:41)

   To what does Jesus contrast hell? (Matthew 25:34)

6. From your study of the following teachings and parables in Matthew, how can we avoid being condemned to hell?

   6:14-15

   13:37-43

   13:47-50

   24:36-51

   25:31-46

7. What does Paul advocate to be the solution? (Romans 5:6-11)

8. From your study of this passage and the previous references, do those who enter hell ever leave? (Luke 16:19-31)

9. From this lesson:

   What warning can you heed?

   What promise has encouraged you?

   What attitude will you change?

   What action will your take?

10. Have you ever been guilty of trying to wish hell away? What has the Lord Jesus been specifically saying to you about the reality of hell in this lesson?

For Further Study
1. Do a research paper on the doctrine of hell for your small group or pastor, using a minimum of 10 reference tools.
2. Read *The Great Divorce* by C.S. Lewis.

•TOOL CHEST•
(A Suggested Optional Resource)

THE GREAT DIVORCE

C.S. Lewis' *The Great Divorce* is a fictitious story of a bus trip from hell to heaven written from the point of view of a passenger. Lewis presents with uncanny insight an imaginative description of hell, driving home hell's reality. He pokes fun at man's attempt to clutch at the beliefs that hell is not quite so bad, nor evil so wrong, and that in good time everything will turn out all right in the end. With great precision and tongue in cheek, his characters act out the many reasons people sadly reject heaven and choose hell. His gripping analogy which someone has termed, "The Lizard's End," depicts the very real and personal battle we wage against the lordship of Christ. This vivid word picture will stay with the readers for years to come.

5
What Is Hell Like?

•FOOD FOR THOUGHT•

The youth group was in full swing. I was talking about the realities of hell to a bunch of lively junior high kids. I wondered if they would be interested. They were! What's more, they came up with some definitions for me. "What do you think hell is really like?" I asked. "I think it's being allowed to take one good look at God and then never being allowed to look again," a 13-year-old boy announced seriously. I think he had one concept of hell right. It is the idea of exclusion from the very presence of God!

The word "hell" means to cover or to hide, and includes the idea of a turning away of the face of the Almighty in revulsion and rejection. Jesus talked about the eternal possibility of God saying, "Depart from Me; I never knew you."

When David's son Absalom rebelled against his father, his insurrection was put down. David allowed him to return and live in Jerusalem, but the Bible says he was not allowed to see the king's face (2 Samuel 14:24-32). Absalom couldn't bear this. To be so close to his father, and yet never allowed to see his face was an exclusion that he couldn't handle. Hell will be like that. Absalom was allowed to see David, but finished up rebelling against him and trying to destroy his own father. He couldn't live with him, and he couldn't live without him. That's hell!

Another word used to describe this place or state is the word *sheol*. It means "to be hollow." Job uses the word *pit* in the Old Testament giving the idea of an empty place beyond death where the dead were gathered in their tribes and families to await the judgment (Genesis 15:15; 49:33; Job 33:24).

Sheol is described as a bottomless, silent space where no bird sings, no child laughs, no wind rustles through the trees. No one talks to anyone for the sense of isolation obsesses the consciousness and locks you into your own lostness. There is also endless boredom and inactivity.

It's hard to describe emptiness, but the Bible tries to help us picture sheol by painting it in shadows and grey tones. C.S. Lewis in *The Great Divorce* pictures an eternal twilight hanging heavy in the damp, moldy air. It is called in the Bible the land of the "shadow" of death. It is in fact like living with everlasting cataracts with unfortunately just enough sight to "see" that there is nothing to see!

Have you ever "dragged" yourself out of a nightmare? Somehow you "know" the horrors are only a dream and it's possible with an incredible effort to wake yourself up. Imagine doing that only to find the nightmare is reality and it's not even possible to escape into sleep again. Think of awaking eternally to bottomless misery.

Jude, verse 12, captures the idea of hell with graphic word pictures. Lost souls are like "clouds without rain," he says, "autumn trees without fruit—uprooted—twice dead!" To die twice—eternally uprooted from all that is dear and familiar—and to die again is to be like "wild waves of the sea foaming up their shame"—with no one to calm the tumult. Hell is being beyond the chance to have Jesus calm the tumultuous sea of fear and dread in our tossing soul!

But it is the last picture in Jude that catches my attention. Jude says lost souls are "orbitless." They are caught in a hellish circuit that isn't a circuit! It doesn't go anywhere! Lost souls are like wandering stars for whom the blackest darkness has been reserved forever. Such orbitless stars are out of control, with no hope of belonging, purpose or usefulness. Who is Jude talking about? Godless men (vv. 4, 7, 19). He urges those who know God and are therefore no longer godless to snatch such people from the fire!

Which brings us to the next word used to describe hell—gehenna. Jesus used this word picture often (Matthew 5:22, 29, 30; 10:28; 18:9; 23:14, 33). Gehenna was the Valley of Hinnom, south of Jerusalem, where humans were once sacrificed and corpses burned (2 Kings 16:3; 21:6). In Jesus' day the refuse of the city was destroyed there, lending itself to a very graphic picture of a fire that is never quenched. Jesus talked of unending pain in this devastating fire (Matthew 25:41; Luke 12:5).

Universalism is a doctrine that offers an alternative theory to the difficulty some people have of believing in hellfire in this day and age. It says that all will eventually be saved. Universalism does for unbelievers what Catholicism holds that purgatory does for believers—that is, fits them for heaven. J.I. Packer in his article "Is Hell Out of Vogue in this Modern Era?" says, "But no form of universalism can stand." He says, "First universalism affirms something of which Scripture gives no hint—second it ignores that which Scripture highlights." Packer says, "Wisdom counsels us to try and imagine what sense of guilt, folly, and loss might lie behind Jesus' horrific images of fire and darkness."

The last word used to describe hell is hades. The place where our disembodied spirits await the judgment. Jesus relates a parable (some think a real account) about a selfish, rich man called Dives (from the Latin for "rich man") who ends up in hell, and a poor man, Lazarus, who was cruelly ignored and ill-treated by the rich man, but who ends up in heaven. He warns about the great gulf fixed between the two and cautions about false hopes of any bridge of belief after death that can span that gulf. Perhaps, as the teenager believed, hell is indeed seeing heaven and knowing that there is no eternal possibility of crossing the canyon between the two. The rich man may appear to be improving as he becomes concerned for the souls of his family, but the main impression from the Scriptures is that of horror at his dilemma, and the helplessness of Abraham or Lazarus himself to alleviate his suffering. Jesus told the story and who can question the truth of it? He also drew our attention to the happiness, comfort, and healing of Lazarus, and the hope and help of those poor in this life, yet rich in faith.

We have been warned. If we have never read the Bible, we have read these pages today. There is no excuse for us. If there is "any doubt in your hearts that you have been saved from such a lost state in the future—you need to make sure of your salvation before this study is over today. Is Christ in your life? Is your sin forgiven for His sake? Ask your group leader to explain how you can be "certain" that Christ is indeed in your heart. The writer to the Hebrews said, "Today if you hear His voice, harden not your heart" (Hebrews 3:15). Today *is* the day of salvation.

•TALKING IT OVER•

1. REVIEW.

   10 Minutes

   Review the four words used for hell. What does each mean?
   ☐ Hell
   ☐ Sheol
   ☐ Gehenna
   ☐ Hades

   Circle the word that taught you something new about hell. Share what that is.

2. READ AND SHARE.

   10 minutes

   Read the Parable of Dives and Lazarus (Luke 16:19-31).
   ☐ Share one thing the parable warns about
   ☐ One thing it promises
   ☐ One thing you want *your* relatives to know

3. FILL IN.

   10 minutes

   Use the acrostics. Fill in with words of warning.

Ghastly	H	H	S
E	E	A	H
H	L	D	E
E	L	E	O
N		S	L
N			
A			

•PRAYING IT THROUGH•

Suggested Times

1. (On your own) Praise God for:
   □ salvation
   □ Christ who purchased it for us
   □ the Holy Spirit who makes it a reality in our lives

   5 Minutes

2. (As a group) Pray for:
   □ preachers to teach it
   □ writers to write it
   □ Sunday School teachers to explain it
   □ Christians to witness to it in a way that will alert people

   5 minutes

3. (As a group) Pray for lost people like Dives:
   □ in your street
   □ in your club
   □ in your church
   □ in your city
   □ in your country

   5 minutes

4. (On your own) Meditate on Luke 16:19-31. Pray quietly for yourself and how you will use the information you are thinking about at your job, in your home, and in your world.

   5 minutes

•DIGGING DEEPER•

1. Look up the following teachings of Jesus on hell.

Gehenna

Matthew 5:22
5:29
5:30
10:28
18:9
23:15
23:33

Mark 9:43
9:45
9:47

Luke 12:5

Hades

Matthew 11:23
16:18

Luke 10:15
16:23

2. Write a brief summary of what Jesus believed and taught about hell.

3. What does Jesus associate with hell?

4. Would Jesus relate hell to the idea of annihilation—to become nonexistent—or describe it as a continuous state? Use scriptural evidence to support your answer.

5. When Jesus speaks of hell, what tone of voice do you perceive He uses from the passages you've studied?

6. See these New Testament references to a future state of condemnation.

   Philippians 3:19
   2 Thessalonians 1:5-9
   2 Timothy 2:12
   Hebrews 10:27, 31
   2 Peter 2

7. Why do you believe these writers were so convinced of the reality of hell?

8. How can you protect yourself and others from an eternal future spent in hell? (cf. Matthew 23:33)

9. What can you do this week to put into practice what you have learned in this lesson?

For Further Study
   1. Memorize 2 Thessalonians 1:8-9.
   2. Read the article on universalism in *Answers to Questions* (Zondervan) by F.F. Bruce.

•TOOL CHEST•
(A Suggested Optional Resource)

ANSWERS TO QUESTIONS

Answers to Questions contains questions on over 200 biblical subjects which have been addressed to F.F. Bruce over the years. A concise answer to each question is provided the reader. Sources are cited when used. Subjects entertained which would increase your understanding of this session would include apostasy, eternity, immortality, judgment, justification, regeneration, salvation, and universalism.

6

The End of the World

•FOOD FOR THOUGHT•

Some people think it's the end of the world on Monday morning; others when their first romance falls apart. Still others believe it's the end of the world when they get a divorce. Some believe sincerely it's the end of all things when a beloved spouse or child dies. But there is another event that the Bible talks about that really *is* the end of everything—the end of the world!

The real end of the world as we know it is first of all delayed by grace. Grace is something we human beings do not deserve one little bit! Grace delays the end of the world. God is waiting because He doesn't want anyone to perish (2 Peter 3:9). The writer of Hebrews having said, "Today is the day of salvation," implies tomorrow it will be too late!

The New Testament Scriptures talk a lot about the last days. In 2 Peter 3:10-14, the apostle says that scoffers will scoff at the very idea of a climactic end to everything. Peter may have been talking to the early gnostics who resisted the idea of a time of judgment and moral accountability, but his words are as relevant today as then.

A *Newsweek* article says, "Missing from most contemporary considerations of heaven is the notion of divine justice" (*Newsweek*, March 27, 1989, p. 53). In fact, the very delay in the coming of these events causes such cynical comments as, "Where *is* the promise of His coming?" The believers' answer to that is it is delayed by God's goodness and grace. He is waiting for us to respond to His good news of salvation.

The Bible says, however, that when the end does come, it will come unexpectedly, "as a thief in the night" (v. 10). We are not therefore to try to fix a date. While Jesus was on earth, even He said He didn't know when all this would take place. This fact should keep us on our toes, watching our lives, and being busy with kingdom work.

Peter says that the "day of the Lord" will come in a catastrophic way, "with great noise, and fervent heat, and the elements will be dissolved" (v. 11). It keeps things in perspective when you realize everything will one day go up in smoke! We need to realize, though, that when God's clock that keeps perfect time strikes midnight, then—and only then—will earthly affairs be culminated. Little people on earth may finger the buttons on a thousand bombs, but only God will press that button in the end. He is, after all, "reserving the world for judgment" (1 Peter 3:7).

All of these certainties should cause us to walk circumspectly—which means like *a cat on hot bricks!* We should be inspired to live whole lives (vv. 11-13). We can also be fully occupied in "hastening His coming." What does this mean?

The Gospel, we are told, must first be preached to every nation, "then will the end come" (Matthew 24:14). So there's lots to do as a third of our world has yet to hear of Christ. Hearing this, some might be tempted to think His Second Coming isn't imminent if so many people still need to hear about His first coming!

At a recent conference, a statement was made concerning Christian radio and the fact that with networking and combined resources, the Gospel could go round the globe in the next 24 hours in the over 200 languages that have already been translated. Within the next 24 hours! In fact, steps are being taken by the major radio ministries to implement that very vision! So who knows how near we are to fulfilling our calling to take the whole Gospel to the whole world?

So Christian service can hasten His kingdom, and so can prayer (Matthew 6:10). In answer to His disciples' request, "Lord, teach us to pray," Christ instructed them to ask that His "kingdom come." If we would only more diligently and fervently pray for the end in a positive sense, I'm sure we would live more productive lives.

In Matthew 24:3, the disciples asked the Lord Jesus what would the signs be of the end of the age. Jesus gave pointers, urging alertness to false christs, faithfulness to endure fears as wars proliferate, and warned that famine would ravage the planet and earthquakes would rock the very foundations of our world. These things He said would be like the first stages of labor! (v. 8)

Christ's disciples will not fare well in this hostile environment, He warned. They will be hated of all nations because of Him. Cults and new religions will abound and deceive even the strongest of Christians; but, said Jesus, "He who will stand firm to the end will be saved." The end of the world will come and we believe soon. Therefore, what manner of people ought we to be?

When the great plants of our cities have turned out
    their last finished work
When the merchants have sold their last yard of silk
    and dismissed their last tired clerk
When the banks have raked in their last shilling
    and paid their last dividend
And the small of the earth say, "Close for the night"
    and asks for a balance . . .
                WHAT THEN??

When the actor has played his last drama
    and the mimic has made his last fun
When the movie has flashed its last picture
    and the billboard displayed its last run
When the crowds seeking pleasure have vanished
    and gone into the darkness again
And a world that's rejected its Saviour
    is asked for an answer . . .
                WHAT THEN??

When the bugle call sinks into silence
    and the long marching columns stand still
When the captain has given his last orders
    and they've captured the last fort and hill
When the flag has been hauled from the masthead
    and the wounded afield checked in
And the trumpet of ages is sounded
    and you stand before Him . . .
                WHAT THEN??

When the people have heard their last sermon
    and the preacher has prayed his last prayer
When the choir has sung its last anthem
    and the sound has died out in the air
When the Bible lies closed on the altar
    and the pews are all empty of men
And each one stands facing his record
    and the great book is opened . . .
                WHAT THEN??

When life, friend, has run to a finish
    When the last thing you can do is done

When your life here on earth is ended
    and eternity's issues begun
As you think of how long God has pleaded
    of how Christ bore your sins on the tree
And your soul stands there naked before Him
    and the Father denies you . . .
                WHAT THEN??

Anonymous

•TALKING IT OVER•

Suggested Times

1. READ AND REVIEW.   *5 minutes*
   Read Matthew 24:1-14 and review the signs of the last days.

2. DISCUSS.   *10 minutes*
   Read II Peter 3. Comment on:
   ☐ What unbelievers forget (v. 5, 8)
   ☐ How the day of the Lord will come like a thief
      (e.g., How does a thief come?)

3. LIST.   *5 minutes*
   In light of the above verses, make a list from verse 11 to the end of the chapter about the sort of people we ought to be, i.e., verse 11—holy people like Him.

4. READ AND MEDITATE.   *10 minutes*
   Read the poem, "What Then" in the text. Are you ready for the end of the world?

•PRAYING IT THROUGH•

Suggested Times

1. (As a group) Praise God for His control of the destiny of:
   - ☐ the world
   - ☐ nations
   - ☐ natural disasters
   - ☐ His people and their eternal safety

8 minutes

2. (As a group) Pray for:
   - ☐ the third of the world that has never once heard of Christ
   - ☐ Christian radio, TV, periodicals
   - ☐ the missionary movement
   - ☐ your own children that they may catch the vision.

8 minutes

3. (On your own) Meditate on 1 Peter 3:11-14. Pray in twos or on your own about these verses.

4 minutes

•DIGGING DEEPER•

You may want to study this lesson in two consecutive weeks doing the overview for week one and 2 Peter 3 for week two.

An Overview of 2 Peter

1. Skim 2 Peter and fill in the charts by titling each passage. Then, using your passage titles for a guide, go back and title each chapter.

2 Peter 1

References	Paragraph Title
vv. 1-2	
vv. 3-11	
vv. 12-21	

2 Peter 2

References	Paragraph Title
vv. 1-3	
vv. 4-10	
vv. 11-22	

2 Peter 3

References	Paragraph Title
vv. 1-2	
vv. 3-7	
vv. 8-13	
vv. 14-18	

2. What does Peter tell us about his readership? (cf. 2 Peter 1:1, 4, 12-13; 3:1)

3. What situations or difficulties were these Christians facing? Support your answer with Scripture references.

4. Review 2 Peter again and identify three or four major purposes of the letter.

5. How does 2 Peter 3 relate or fit in with the whole book?

6. The emphasis on Christ's return serves as a warning and as an incentive. Explain this statement using examples from Peter's work.

2 Peter 3

7. What, according to Peter, is his purpose in writing this letter? (cf. 3:1)

   What makes for wholesome thinking? Would you describe your thought life as wholesome?

8. Peter placed the Apostles on the same plane as the Old Testament prophets as authoritative communicators of God's truth. The scoffers evidently were casting doubt on the Apostles and their message. What precise teaching(s) of the Apostles were being ridiculed by these cynics? (cf. 3:3-7)

   What two arguments does Peter offer to prove their accusations false? (vv. 5-8)

9. Define the two contrasts in verse 9 and explain what the Lord's delay provides (cf. 2 Peter 3:15; 1 Timothy 2:4).

10. Peter quotes Jesus saying, "The day of the Lord will come like a thief" in the night (cf. Matthew 24:43-44; Luke 12:39-40).

How would you characterize a thief's coming? Give a personal example if you can.

11. Verses 11-18 serve as the "so whats" to the certainty of coming judgment. What are they? Pinpoint one you will dedicate yourself to pray for and concentrate on this week.

12. What should the thought of Christ's return bring us? (v. 14)

13. How does Peter support all he has just said (the certainty and description of coming judgment, the purpose for the delay, the lifestyle those who anticipate Christ's return should cultivate, and the attitudes we should emulate in light of eternity)? (vv. 15-16)

    2 Peter 3:15; Romans 2:4; 3:25; 9:22; 11:22

    2 Peter 3:16

14. Peter concludes (v. 18) by coming back to his main theme of 2 Peter, the importance of our growing in knowledge of Christ (cf. 1:2, 5, 8, 12; 2:3, 12, 20; 3:18). What is something specific you could do to get to know Jesus better?

15. What are some of the signs Peter mentions as forerunners to the day of the Lord?

16. Disbelief in the Lord's return results in what according to 2 Peter 2?

17. How many times in 2 Peter 3 does Peter emphasize judgment and destruction? What should this tell us?

18. How will Christ's return affect men's eternal destinies? How will He find you when He comes again?

For Further Study
1. Make a list of the characteristics of the false teachers and scoffers in 2 Peter. Do any of these describe you? (i.e., Do you struggle with cynicism?) Make a commitment to a friend to pray daily for yourself in weak areas of your life.
2. Memorize 2 Peter 3:8-9.

•TOOL CHEST•
(A Suggested Optional Resource)

COMMENTARIES ON 2 PETER

Studying Peter's second epistle may raise many questions in the Bible student's mind. After doing your own inductive work like what you have done on the Digging Deeper section of session 6, you will probably want to consult a commentary or two with your list of questions. This is appropriate now that you have a thorough and firsthand understanding of 2 Peter. Remember, good Bible students are not necessarily those who think they know the most, but those who approach the Scriptures with an inquisitive mind, full of questions, and as if it were the first time they had read them. A few commentaries for your consideration are: Michael Green's *The Second Epistle General of Peter and the General Epistle of Jude: An Introduction and Commentary* (The Tyndale New Testament Commentaries, Wm. B. Eerdmans Publishing Company); J.N.D. Kelly's *A Commentary on the Epistles of Peter and Jude*, (Thornapple Commentaries, Baker Book House).

7

The Great White Throne

•FOOD FOR THOUGHT•

So what happens *after* the end of the world? Hebrews 9:27 says, "As it is appointed unto men once to die, and after that the judgment." There *is* an "after that"! What happens then is depicted for us in Revelation 20:11-15.

John tells us the throne of God is a *great* throne. It speaks of power, authority, and justice. He says it is a white throne; that gives us an idea of the white hot holiness of God. And John also saw the dead, great and small standing before this awesome throne ready for judgment.

After God intervenes in human history and brings it to a close, He alone determines the eternal fate of people. He places them in surroundings specially adapted to their final condition.

First of all, we need to understand that judgment is a compliment. A child that is never punished feels his or her actions have no consequence! In other words, the little one says, "If my acts are worth evaluating, I am of value. If what I *do* matters—what I *am* matters!" Adults need to realize that too.

Secondly, judgment is right! It's *right* that wrongs are righted, that injustice is dealt with by a righteous judge. God, we believe, is that right judge. We can certainly know that a righteous God will do the right thing in that day. "Shall not the Judge of all the world do right?" the Scriptures ask (Genesis 18:25). And again the Scriptures affirm, "Lord, true and righteous are Thy judgments" (Revelation 19:2).

Thirdly, God will judge the world by Jesus Christ. When Christ walked among men, He gave them a chance to meet Him as Saviour. That chance pertains today. After we die, we shall meet Him as Judge! There *is* a resurrection that leads to judgment rather than life. "When the Son of Man comes in His glory, and all the angels with Him, He will sit on His throne in heavenly glory. All the nations will be gathered before Him, and He will separate the people one from another as a shepherd separates the sheep from the goats. He will put the sheep on His right and the goats on His left. . . . Then they will go away to eternal punishment, but the righteous to eternal life" (Matthew 25:31-33, 46). The vivid Bible imagery pictures the severity of the punishment that awaits those judged for their sin that has not been forgiven here and now.

The Word tells us that the dead will be judged out of "the books." Which books are these? Records of lives lived with or without Christ. They are described as the books of the dead. In these books the things they have done are recorded. We don't need to wait and see if the scales of justice will fall in our favor. We can know now no amount of good things that we have done will do because the things we have not done (and the things we wished we had done) will far outweigh the little good that we can muster. As that convicting record is read out in the presence of all the angels and all the dead, small and great, another book will be opened. This book is called the Book of Life (Rev. 20:15). It is the record of redemption.

So the questions arise, how do you get your name written in the Book of Life—in the record of redemption? Because if the angel cannot find your name, you will share the fate of the lost. The answer is quite simple.

You ask Jesus to write it in now—while you are still alive! You cast yourself on the mercy of God and thank Him for what He has done for you! You realize you could never do enough to merit heaven and you acknowledge that God is the only One who can blot out the record of your wrongs. The book is His as heaven is His!

Don't wait till God judges the lost to find out if your name has been included in the Lamb's Book of Life. It is too late then. Listen to this frightening prophecy. "The sea gave up the dead that were in it, and death and Hades gave up the dead that were in them; and each person was judged according to what he had done. Then death and Hades were thrown into the lake of fire. The lake of fire is the second death. If anyone's name was not found written in the book of life, he was thrown into the lake of fire" (Revelation 20:13-15).

The second death awaits those who reject God's Christ who is the only way to heaven. But life as we have never and can never even imagine awaits those who come in faith and repentance to Him now.

> Rock of Ages cleft for me,
> Let me hide myself in Thee;

Let the water and the blood,
From Thy riven side which flowed,
Be of sin the double cure,
Cleanse me from its guilt and pow'r.

Not the labors of my hands
Can fulfill Thy law's demands;
Could my zeal no respite know,
Could my tears forever flow,
All for sin could not atone;
Thou must save and Thou alone.

Nothing in my hand I bring,
Simply to Thy cross I cling;
Naked, come to Thee for dress,
Helpless, look to Thee for grace;
Foul, I to the fountain fly,
Wash me, Saviour, or I die!

While I draw this fleeting breath,
When my eyes shall close in death,
When I soar to worlds unknown,
See Thee on Thy judgment throne,
Rock of Ages cleft for me,
Let me hide myself in Thee.

Amen.

Revelation 22:13-14 tells me that the Holy Spirit works tirelessly to ensure my safe passage into the arms of God. The church exists to preach the Good News that there is a way of escape for all of us. The Word of God assures us that Jesus came "to seek and to save that which was lost" (Luke 19:10).

In a letter from World Relief, I read this story of a little Vietnamese boy. He was standing by the bedside of his sister—a very sick little girl.

He was wearing of all things, a T-shirt with Batman emblazoned on the front. Through the nurse, my friend asked if he knew who that was.

The tyke nodded and said, "Batman."

And then he added, "Batman is going to come and make my sister better."

At my desk half a world away, that lad's simple faith has touched me. He didn't know about Jesus, but he knew that it would take somebody bigger than himself to help his little sister.

But you and I know there are no superheroes to rescue the little children of the world from disease, hunger, suffering and poverty.

Thinking about that sad little boy and his totally misplaced hope, I add my comment to the letter: "We know there are no superheroes to rescue such children from hell either—save Jesus! He is no false hope. He is able to save because He is God. And He is able because He loves all of us and wants us to be with Him forever."

•TALKING IT OVER•

1. READ AND DISCUSS IN TWOS.

   10 minutes

   ☐ Read Revelation 20:11-15. What do you find hard to believe? Easy to accept?

   ☐ Work in twos. One of you be an unbeliever, the other a Christian. How would the Christian explain this passage to the unbeliever?

   ☐ The little Vietnamese boy believed Batman would save his sister. Who do people in our culture believe will save them today?

2. DISCUSS.

   10 minutes

   Read Revelation 22:12-17.

   ☐ How does Christ describe Himself and what do you think this means? (v. 12)

   ☐ What contrasts are given in verse 14?

   ☐ What are the things Jesus has done in order to stop us from going to hell? (v. 16)

   ☐ What is the message of the Holy Spirit and the Church? (v. 17)

3. EXAMINE THE WARNING.

   10 minutes

   Revelation 22:18 contains a warning. What is it? How does this warning pertain to this lesson?

•PRAYING IT THROUGH•

Suggested Times

1. (As a group) Praise God that Jesus can be known as Saviour now. — *2 minutes*

2. (As a group) Praise God for the person, church, TV show, book, etc., that explained this Good News to you. — *3 minutes*

3. (In twos) Pray diligently and intensely for people you know who have not come to Christ. — *7 minutes*

4. (As a group) Pray for gospel messengers: — *7 minutes*
   □ pastors
   □ Sunday School teachers
   □ evangelists
   □ Christian writers
   □ Radio and TV ministries
   □ Christian drama
   □ Christian schools and universities

5. (On your own) Pray for yourself and your own responsibility to share the Good News of salvation. — *1 minute*

•DIGGING DEEPER•

Again, due to the length of this study you may wish to tackle it in two weeks.

Judgment

1. A common theme in Scripture is God presented as judge. Look up these references and make notes of their content.

   Genesis 18:25

   Deuteronomy 1:17

   Deuteronomy 32:4

   Psalm 9:8

   Psalm 94:2

   Isaiah 30:18

   Ezekiel 7:27

   Romans 1:18

   Romans 3:5-6

   Hebrews 12:23

   1 Peter 1:17

   1 Peter 2:23

   Revelation 16:5

2. From your study thus far, what is associated with the judgment of God? (also cf. Psalm 36:5-6; Ezekiel 39:21ff)

3. Who is pictured in Scripture as sometimes carrying out God's judgment? How can we reconcile this with the passages we read previously which present God as judge?

   John 5:22

   John 5:28-30

   John 9:39

   Acts 10:42

   Acts 17:31

   2 Timothy 4:8

4. According to the following references, who will come under the judgment of God?

   1 Corinthians 3:12-15

   1 Corinthians 5:10

   2 Timothy 4:1

   Hebrews 12:23

   1 Peter 4:5

   2 Peter 2:4

   Jude 6

5. Will Christians escape God's judgment?

   Hebrews 10:30

   James 3:1

   1 Peter 1:17

   1 Peter 4:17

Revelation 20:12

What will the results of judgment entail for the faithful? The wicked? To others mentioned? (cf. Exodus 6:6; Numbers 33:4; Deuteronomy 10:18; 32:41; Psalm 25:9-10; Isaiah 4:4; Jeremiah 4:12ff)

6. Summarize what you have learned so far about our just God and His judgment.

The Final Judgment

7. To what is the future and final judgment of God linked?

OT	NT
Joel 2:1ff	Matthew 25:31-46
Amos 5:18ff	John 6:39-40
Obadiah 15	1 Corinthians 4:3-5

8. Can His judgment be avoided? (Romans 2:3; Hebrews 10:26-31)

9. On what basis will each individual be judged and accepted or rejected by God? (Matthew 11:21-24; 25:31-46; Romans 2:12-16; 5:15-19)

Revelation 20:11-15

10. Read Revelation 20:11-15. John employs poetic imagery to depict the future final judgment in order to get across what idea to his readers in verse 11?

"Great White Throne"

"Earth and sky fled from His presence"

11. What is the tone of the passage?

12. Who is seated on the throne here? How does this fit with your observations on question 3? (cf. Matthew 25:31; Revelation 5:13)

13. To whom does "great and small" refer? Why does John use more images in verse 13 to the sea giving up its dead and of death and Hades giving up their dead? What is his major concept?

14. Look up the definition of Hades in a Bible dictionary. Are only the wicked awaiting judgment there? In verse 14 death and Hades are personified. What is John portraying by his word-picture?

15. How many books are opened and what information does each contain? What is the basis of judgment in each?

16. What will happen to those whose names are written in the Book of Life? To those whose names are not recorded? Is anyone saved by his works recorded in the other books?

17. Where will the end of the world find you?

For Further Study
1. What do these parables teach us about judgment?
2. Choose a Scripture passage from this lesson that you found enlightening and commit it to memory.

•TOOL CHEST•
(A Suggested Optional Resource)

POCKET GUIDE TO THE BIBLE

A Pocket Guide to the Bible (C. Bridgeland and Francis Foulkes, IVP) is a brief summary of every book of the Bible. When you are cross-referencing or consulting a text in an unfamiliar portion of Scripture, this tool is useful in gaining a quick understanding to the background of your passage. It will introduce you to each book's purpose, theme, outline, and content. Other pertinent works on that particular book are noted at the end of each chapter. You might consult this tool when looking up the many passages under the Judgment and Final Judgment sections of this study to acquaint yourself with the context surrounding an individual verse.

8

The Judgment Seat of Christ

•FOOD FOR THOUGHT•

Sometimes someone will ask, "Will Christians be judged if they have accepted Christ?" The answer is very easy—Yes. Paul says to the Christians at Rome, "You, then, why do you judge your brother? Or why do you look down on your brother? For we will all stand before God's judgment seat. It is written: 'As surely as I live,' says the Lord, 'every knee will bow before Me; every tongue will confess to God.' So then, each of us will give an account of himself to God" (Philippians 2:10). The Bible doesn't say we will all stand before the Judgment Seat *except me!* We are to leave the judging to Christ, realizing we shall all answer to Him.

So what shall we be judged for? Our sin? No, fortunately! Our works since we came to know Christ. Paul tells the Corinthians that He laid down a good foundation for their faith by sound doctrine and now they are to add the building blocks of good works on that firm foundation. On the day of judgment the quality of those good things we are supposed to do will be tested. There will be an evaluation. We are not saved by works, but we are saved "unto" the good works God has prepared for us (Ephesians 2:10).

Paul uses the figure of fire to describe how searing that divine evaluation will be! It will burn up worthless work like wood, hay, or straw. On the other hand, the test of divine judgment will leave any of the pure teaching we have built into our lives and our wholesome living intact. Paul says some Christians will find themselves losing everything except their very souls. In other words, they will be saved—but only by the skin of their teeth (1 Corinthians 3:10-15). As an old couplet puts it:

Only One life twill soon be past
Only what's done for Christ will last.

In 2 Corinthians 5:10 Paul says, "For we must *all* appear before the Judgment Seat of Christ, that each one may receive what is due him for the things done while in the body, whether good or bad."

This judgment has nothing whatsoever to do with justification which is credited to the believer through faith in his Saviour—it refers only to the things we have done or have committed ourselves to doing since we came to faith. This evaluation is not for punishment, but rather for reward. After this divine evaluation, our Saviour will say to some, "Well done, thou good and faithful servant," which will be the grandest reward of all.

It would certainly not be right that those who have labored for Christ so diligently and at great cost should not be rewarded. Some might say, "But doesn't the Bible say, 'Everlasting joy will crown their heads'? (Isaiah 35:10; 51:11) Surely this should be enough!" Yes, it does say that. It also promises rest from our labors and a new body fitted ideally for its new environment; not to mention the reward of being with the people we love who have preceded us to heaven. But beside all these unmerited gifts of God's grace, the Bible also speaks of other rewards.

The biblical picture is that of a crown. Paul says, "Now there is in store for me the crown of righteousness, which the Lord, the righteous Judge, will award me on that day—and not only to me, but also to all who have longed for His appearing." The Scriptures talk of rewards for endurance and even a special reward for those who look for His appearing (2 Timothy 4:8). There will be a crowning reward from the hand of Christ for the fighter, the faith keeper. There will also be a reward for the evangelist. "Those who are wise will shine like the brightness of the heavens, and those who lead many to righteousness, like the stars for ever and ever" (Daniel 12:3).

But the whole tenor of Scripture encourages us to love Christ supremely and serve Him wholeheartedly, not looking for compensation or reward, but simply for the sheer joy of serving Jesus!

When I first became a Christian and learned about all these rewards—the "crowns" that God would give to His faithful people—I determined to "go for the gold!" I fondly imagined myself arriving in heaven, being greeted by a grateful God, and having my glowing brow piled high with crowns interspersed with halos! The idea suited me well, and I set about making sure it happened. It was not long before I realized it was not going to be as easy as I had thought!

Having received the crown of life, (Revelation 2:10), I became aware of my many, many shortcomings (commonly called *sins!*) and ended up flat on my face, tripped up by my own tainted ambition after I had hardly set off from the starting line!

Alas, if I made it in any category at all, it would only be because of His help, His forgiveness, His power, and His enabling! Therefore, the crowns He would give me would not even belong to me, but rather to Him!

It was with a much subdued spirit I came across Revelation 4:10 in my daily Bible reading. Now I came to understand what any crown I might receive was for. It was to have something in my heavenly hands to cast at His heavenly feet! How terrible to stand before Him empty-handed in that day!

When Paul talked of the Judgment Seat of Christ, he was writing to the Corinthians (2 Corinthians 5:10). He knew they had been there at the time he had been dragged before the "bema"—the judgment seat at Corinth to defend himself before the Roman proconsul, Gallio (Acts 18:12ff).

The Corinthians got the message. Have we? "We shall *all* stand before the bema of Christ in heaven" as Paul stood before the bema on earth. Do we understand this? It was a sobering message then— and it is a sobering message now. I don't know about you, but when my turn comes, I want to have something in my hands!

THE JUDGMENT SEAT

When I stand at the Judgment Seat of Christ
    and He shows me His plan for me,
the plan of my life as it might have been,
    had He had His way, and I see,
how I blocked Him here, and checked Him there
    and would not yield my will—
Shall I see grief in my Saviour's eyes
    Grief though He loves me still?
He would have me rich, but I
    stand there poor, stripped of all but His grace . . .
while my memory runs like a hunted thing down the
    paths I can't retrace.
Then my desolate heart will well nigh break
    with tears that I cannot shed,
I'll cover my face with my empty hands,
    and bow my uncrowned head.

No, Lord of the life that's left to me,
I yield it to Thy hand. Take me, make me, mold me,
to the pattern Thou has planned.

Anonymous

•TALKING IT OVER•

1. DISCUSS FREELY.

☐ Did you realize that Christians will be judged one day?

☐ What is that judgment for?

☐ What do you feel about such rewards and what are they for?

2. SHARE WITH PARTNERS.

Look up all these Scriptures and choose one that speaks in a meaningful way to you. Share it with your partner.

☐ Romans 14:10-12

☐ 1 Corinthians 3:10-15

☐ 2 Corinthians 5:10

3. READ AND DISCUSS.

Read Revelation 4. Make a list of heavenly rewards that wait for us.

☐ Why do you think the 24 elders cast their crowns before the throne?

☐ What one thought from this lesson will change your life?

•PRAYING IT THROUGH•

Suggested Times

1. (As a group) Write a thank-You note to God for some of the rewards He has given you already. Read them to the group.

   5 minutes

2. (On your own) Write an apology for the "bad works" you are aware of. Silently pray as you read your apology to God.

   5 minutes

3. (On your own) Write a request for a Christian you know who looks as though he or she will have empty hands in heaven. Pray for him or her [no names].

   5 minutes

4. (On your own) Write a promise to God about the "good works" you will begin today. Finish with a general time of praise.

   5 minutes

•DIGGING DEEPER•

1. Romans 14:10 clearly states that everyone will stand before God's judgment seat and give an account of himself/herself. See the surrounding context and determine who this Scripture is addressed to and why?

2. On what basis does this passage imply Christians will be judged?

3. According to the following references, what other aspects of our lives will God judge?

   Matthew 12:36

   Matthew 25:14-30

   Matthew 25:31-46

   Romans 2:16

   1 Corinthians 4:5

   1 Peter 1:17

   Revelation 20:12

4. How do these Scriptures characterize the judgment of Christians?

   1 Peter 1:17

   1 Corinthians 3:13

5. What is the purpose of God's judgment on believers? (1 Corinthians 4:5; 2 Corinthians 5:10)

6. The Bible reveals that the Lord Jesus will exercise God's judgment on Christians at the judgment seat of Christ. From your study of what that judgment will be based on, how do you think you will fare?

7. What changes must you make by the Lord's enabling to be presentable before His judgment seat?

In motive: In relationships:

In attitude: In responsibilities

In speech: In stewardship:

In conduct: In opportunities:

For Further Study
1. Memorize 2 Corinthians 5:10.
2. Review the Digging Deeper studies in this book and make a report of what you have learned about heaven and hell, summarizing each study in a paragraph or two. Share it with a friend.

•TOOL CHEST•
(A Suggested Optional Resource)

HYMNALS

In this chapter we saw the 24 Elders in the Book of Revelation laying their crowns before the throne worshiping the Lord in praise and song (cf. Revelation 4:10-11; 5:8-14). Hymns are expressions of adoration to our triune God. They are rich in theology telling God back who He is and what He has done for His people. Based on Scripture, they open our eyes to the truth of a Bible passage and show us its relevancy to our every day living.

Keep your favorite hymnal with your frequently used Bible study tools. Use it often to refresh your personal devotions and to deepen your understanding of God's Word. Why not try singing the hymn "Man of Sorrows" in your small group this week at the end of your lesson to help the group reflect on the precious reality and costliness of the gift of heaven and eternal life which you have been freely given.

"Man of Sorrows," what a name
For the Son of God who came
Ruined sinners to reclaim!
Hallelujah! what a Savior!

Bearing shame and scoffing rude,
In my place condemned He stood;
Sealed my pardon with His blood:
Hallelujah! what a Savior!

Guilty vile and helpless, we:
Spotless Lamb of God was He:
"Full atonement!" can it be?
Hallelujah! what a Savior!

"Lifted up" was He to die,
"It is finished," was His cry;
Now in heav'n exalted high:
Hallelujah! what a Savior!

When He comes, our glorious King,
All His ransomed home to bring,
Then anew this song we'll sing:
Hallelujah! what a Savior!